ALL THE PRINCIPALITY OF MONACO

10th Edition, June 1990

I.S.B.N. 84-378-0361-6

Dep. Legal B. 22119-1990

editorial escudo de oro, s.a. Palaudarias, 26 - 08004 Barcelona - Spain

Impreso en España - Printed in Spain
FISA - ESCUDO DE ORO, S.A. - Palaudarias, 26 - Barcelona (Spain)

In this old engraving of Monaco we can see the fortress of the Grimaldi as the navigators of old might have seen it from the sea.

MONACO

The ancient navigators were true masters in the art of giving names to the unknown lands they came upon on their journeys. They named different regions and countries according to their fruits, climate or geographical position; as for example, The Garden of Oranges, The Land of Silver, and The Islands of the Storm. Then, history began to change these names until their flowery poetic aroma disappeared completely.

It is said that the name Monaco comes from *Portus Monoeci,* the old port of Hercules quoted in Mediterranean legends. But Monaco should really be named Haven of Calm, Land of the Sun, and Garden of Happiness. Like a white seagull, she flies between sea and sky, playing with the murmur of sea foam and champagne bubbles with an infectious feminine gaiety. Wearing pink and blue flowers at her breast, she runs barefoot over the bitter virile fields smelling of rosemary, lemon and the sea.

The Principality of Monaco is made up of three districts, these being the old community of Monaco, presided over by the noble pile of the palace of the Grimaldi; the Condamine, port area; and Monte-Carlo, the rock with the casino, the hotels, and never-ending parties. The new district of ''Fontvieille'', an area of almost 220.000 m² reclaimed from the sea, will also be incorporated.

There is a long and interesting history under this gay optimistic surface. This is one of Monaco's best kept secrets, she has been able to convert her history into life and her roots have given fruit. In the environs of Monaco there are many historical remains, and in the caves are preserved the skeletons of the first inhabitants of the Mediterranean, and the remains of old cyclopic walls are to be seen on the hills. This is, without any doubt, the land quoted by Virgil and

Lucan: an impregnable fortress, calm port "where the strength of the Eurus and the Zephyr does not reach". Occasionally the waters give back a piece of this history from a shipwreck in the deep in the shape of a Carthaginian coin, remains of Phoenician pottery, a Greek sword... All the sea-faring people of the Mediterranean sailed through these waters and stayed in these lands.

In the year 43 B.C. Caesar concentrated his fleet in the port of Monaco and waited in vain for the arrival of Pompey who was taking refuge in Illyria. After this date, for many centuries, the name of Monaco did

The coat of arms of Monaco over the main door of the Palace. Below, an overall view of the Principality in which its three main districts can clearly be seen: to the right — Monaco; in the centre, the port area of La Condamine; to the left, Monte-Carlo.

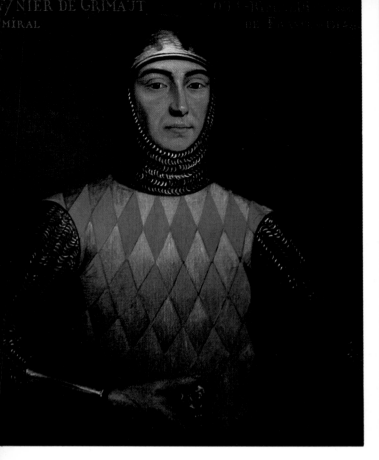

not often appear in literary texts, but in the 12th century, Frederick Barbarossa, Emperor of Germany, conceded Genoa the sovereignty of the whole Ligurian coast, from Porto Venere to Monaco. These were the years the struggle between Guelfs (partisans of the Pope) and Ghibellines (the supporters of the Emperor). And it was at that time too when an old Ligurian family named Grimaldi began to achieve eminence in the history of Genoa: able businessmen as behoves worthy representatives of the valient Mediterranean races, the Grimaldi were also astute politicians, and several consuls and Genoese embassadors bore that name.

The Grimaldi belonged to the Guelf faction, and faithful to their party were obliged to accept the bitter road to exile when in 1295 the Ghibellines gained control in Genoa. Rainier Grimaldi died in the defence of his lost cause having become captain of a brave fleet of ships that gave chase to all Genoese ships on the Ligurian coastline. Another of this relations, Francesco Grimaldi, succeeded in capturing the rock of Monaco. This is a picturesque page from history, as Francesco Grimaldi disguised himself as a friar in order to get into the fortress. And so with a ruse worthy of Ulysses himself, he succeeded in surprising the Genoese garrison, thus acquiring the nickname with which he has gone down in history —"Malizia".

As from this time, the Grimaldi gradually acquired a stronger hold over the rock, which they had to de-

Several generations of the Grimaldi family joined by history: on the left, Rainier I, admiral of France and a brave soldier. On the right, Louis II, who fought for peace when Europe was devastated by World War II. On the following page, H.S.H. Prince Rainier III, the present sovereign of Monaco and his future successor crown Prince Albert.

Aerial view of the Principality of Monaco.

fend, sometimes heroically, from the ambitions of Genoa and Savoy. In 1506 the Monegasques withstood a four month long siege by a Genoan army ten times their size. Luciano Grimaldi, Lord of Monaco, showed his bravery on this occasion.

But although the Grimaldi had been obliged to become soldiers, they had not lost their traditional intelligence in the sphere of politics and human relations. When subjected in 1509 to French sovereignty, they were able enough to approach the Spanish sphere of influence. The Treaties of Burgos and Tordesillas (1524) recognized the full autonomy of this small state. Augustin Grimaldi, bishop of Grasse, was placed at the head of the government. Thus a

tiny state was born which had as its protector the most powerful monarch in Christendom —the Emperor Charles V. This same Emperor stayed in the castle for three days in the year 1529 on the occasion of one of his journeys to Italy.

But the Grimaldi's did not wish to remain for ever under Spanish tutelage in a prolonged and lazy infancy. Honoré II —who was the first to bear the title of Prince—, showing subtle awareness, signed a secret treaty with Richelieu in 1641. After this, the Princes of Monaco enjoyed the protection of France and even lived at the court of this friendly country. These were the good years of the last of the Louis and no one could foresee the coming of the Revolution when all

Europe was astounded by the happenings in Paris. Honoré III, Prince of Monaco, was dethroned and imprisoned in Paris. The Principality seemed to be floundering in the lands of its new masters. Then the Treaty of Vienna placed Monaco under the protection of Sardinia; Menton and Roquebrune being separated from it, thus reducing the already small area of the country. Monaco remained under Sardinian protection until 1860 when, being weak and dismembered, it was placed once more under the protection of France.

This tragic moment in its history and these difficult years were, however, decisive for the future of the Principality. Prince Charles III of the Grimaldi devoted his whole life to the reconstruction of his country, and under his able rule, Monaco became a modern country, open to the most progressive influences and ideas of the period. His son Prince Albert I, an eminent scientist and seaman, consolidated the task of reconstruction. Relations with France were amicably established and Monaco, thanks to the personal talents of its sovereign, became a key point in cultural life in the Mediterranean. Now, its prestige as a tourist resort is added to its fame as an international centre for cultural occasions of all kinds. Prince Louis II, son of Prince Albert I, had a difficult time during

A view of the Principality with the new districts developing on the coast and the mountainside.

the Second World War, and these years also helped to form his successor, the present Prince Rainier III who faithfully continued the social work and the promotion of new entreprises which have made the Principality into the prosperous, optimistic, and peaceful spot we know today. With the help of his wife, Princess Grace, the reigning monarch of Monaco has succeeded in projecting an open, dynamic, image of this country.

Princes of this white seagull playing on the sea shore, the sovereigns of Monaco and their people have brought about a real story-book situation of a better world with their faith and affection, for the name of Monaco is never used today in connexion with an argument or any type of violence. Like a lingering perfume, the name of Monaco is whispered in moments of pleasure and love and ideal journeys to the land of happiness.

The Principality of Monaco is a land in which the flowers of peace grow freely, and neither wars nor the passing of centuries have succeeded in taking this privileged state from the hands or the heart of the Grimaldi family.

On these pages, different views of the Monaco Palace, built on the site of a fortress constructed by the Genoese in 1215.

THE GRIMALDI PALACE

The Grimaldi Palace, with its solid square aspect is a fine symbol of the tenacity which has distinguished the Grimaldi family for centuries. It is also a real museum with fine furniture decorating its apartments. The palace dates from the 16th and 17th centuries but still preserves its mediaeval towers, built by the Genoese in 1215. Francesco Grimaldi took possession of the fortress in 1297, and his successors enlarged it, converting it into a noble mansion capable of housing even the Emperor Charles V.

Honoré II was of course the great renovator of the family castle and it was he who organized the distribution of the apartments inside. The fountains and gardens are also attributed to the creative impulse of this same Prince. As a lover of the arts and letters, Honoré II owned nearly 700 paintings signed by the greatest masters. The historian Juan Le Laboureur, who stayed at the palace in 1646, has left

The Prince's Palace.

The changing of the guard at the Palace is an attractive spectacle for many people who congregate on the esplanade to get a good view of the soldiers.

GALERIE D'HERCULE

some impressions of this fabulous art collection. Honoré II, the humanist prince, created his tiny Versailles, a satin and velvet court of silver and ebony.

On the left, the Gallery of Hercules, where the Renaissance decoration of the palace can be seen in all its splendour. Above these lines, the Mazarino Room with its elegant ornamentation. Over the chimney is a portrait of Cardinal Mazarino painted in the 17th century by an artist of the French school.

The storm of the Revolution engulfed these melancholy memories and devastated a large part of the princes' residence. After this, many years were needed to rebuild the old palace. Finally, it was the present sovereign, H.S.H. Prince Rainer III, who succeeded in restoring the building, giving back its old refined splendour. With exquisite taste he has changed the parquet flooring for one of Italian marble decorated with the orignal designs. Thanks to this great work of reconstruction, the visitor to the palace can marvel at the elegance and refinement of its rooms.

On the initiative of the present monarch there has been created a new wing of the palace which comprises numerous private rooms and also an interesting Napoleonic Museum that preserves many reminiscences of the Grimaldi family. In these rooms the Grimaldi dynasty pays homage to the Emperor Napoleon.

The harmony of line and the beauty of the many canvases by famous painters decorating the rooms and chambers in the Palace are an enviable inheritance. Among the names of the great masters whose works can be seen by the visitor are: Nicolas and Pierre Mignard, Giorgine, Lebrun, Holbein, J. B. van Loo, Philippe de Champaigne, H. Rigaud, J. Bressan,

The Blue Room. The walls are decorated in Louis XIV style, matching with the furniture in gilded wood. The lamps are of Venetian cut crystal. On the right is a portrait of Maria Leczinska, the wife of Louis XV King of France, painted by Stiemart.

The Throne Room. Especially outstanding are the frescoes by Orazio Ferrari framing the throne, topped by the arms of the House of Grimaldi. The chandeliers made from Polish crystal provide the finishing touch to this majestic room.

Pierre Gobert, etc. But one of the most interesting rooms, both in the quality of its furnishings and paintings, and in the historic legend surrounding it is the York Room. It was where, towards the end of the 18th century, the Duke of York breathed his last. The bed, the balustrade and the framework of the bed place are decorated with gilt carvings of the 17th century. Venetian objects and Japanese furniture, and a frescoed ceiling with ''Fame with the coat of arms of the Grimaldi'' in the centre, painted in 1688 by Gregorio di Ferrari, give this room an exceptionally artistic quality.

Its legend is summarized as follows and has its origin in the stories of the fishermen who threw the nets at the Point of the Veille, east of Monaco. In the 18th century, the Duke of York, brother of George III king of England, was obliged to abandon his ship off the coast of the Principality, and requested help from the Lord of Monaco. The Duke of York became ill and died in this room in the Prince's Palace. Then the fishermen said that during his illness and until his death, a woman dressed in white appeared on the Point de la Veille every day and spent hours staring towards the Palace. When the funeral barge bearing the body of the Duke of York went out of sight, the white goddess gave a shrill piercing cry and cast herself into the waves never to return. Legend becomes confused with history and the Grimaldi Palace is no exception to this and plays an important part in our history.

The Officers' Room.

The Louis XV Room.

The York bed-room with its interesting picture collection.

Louis XV bed-room, decorated towards the end of the 18th century. The bed, with a Polish style canopy is made of carved gilt wood.

THE NAPOLEONIC MUSEUM

Prince Louis II, General of the French army, had, during his reign, gathered together with ability and enthusiasm, a collection of Napoleonic memorabilia of great quality.

H.S.H. Prince Rainier III has not only added to the collection but also tried to give it a framework worthy of its attractive historical value.

These Napoleonic relics which are now on view to the public are in the recently built south wing of the Palace; and in the upper rooms of this wing are the collections of the Palace Archives, where thousands of documents related to the past of the Principality

On the left, the Gallery of Mirrors. On the right the Saint John the Baptist Chapel built in 1656.

can be examined. Visitors can also admire the collections of coins minted by the Princes of Monaco since 1640, original letters of Charles V, Cardinal Richelieu and Louis XIV, and a collection of the postage stamps issued by the Principality since the reign of Charles III.

The striking uniforms of the Prince's Guards through the centuries, old engravings, pictures of Monaco through the ages, the Napoleonic Museum, the collections of the Palace Archives etc. allow visitors and those fond of the history of France and Monaco to become acquainted with these prestigious souvenirs that honour both the past and the illustrious home of the Grimaldi.

The Napoleonic Museum, where there is a valuable collection of objects reminiscent of the Emperor.

THE SEA — THE HEART OF MONACO

In addition to its age-old traditions, to the refined modernity of Monte-Carlo, so redolent of the *Belle Epoque,* to an active artistic and cultural life and intense social activity, there is also the sea. The sea, with its limpid azure presence, a perfect backcloth for a truly marvellous setting.

Castles of fireworks are set off from the sea, and it is in the sea where everyone enjoys the healthy pleasure of a sporting life. The thousands of boats of all shapes and sizes gently rock on these calm tranquil waters. The weather and the sun are a further natural attraction. The climate is mild with an average annual temperature of 16° 31 — and 2,583 hours of sunshine annually.

The Rock of Monaco.

The installations in La Condamme port.

The sea, with its considerable store of life beneath its waters has benefitted from the initiative of the Monaco Government and the Monegasque Association for the Protection of Nature, which have made it possible for there to be space devoted to the preservation of flora and fauna. In the Gulf of Larvotto, in an area cordoned off by buoys and out of bounds to ships and fishermen is this "sacred space" of silence. The sea is an immutable presence, the very heart of the Monegasque coast.

Two views of the rock of Monaco where the palace is situated.

A view of the port of Monaco under a blue sky.

The port of Fontvieille at the foot of the rock.

The yellow, white and ochre maze of the streets of old
Monaco, flanked by shops.

Saint Nicholas square. ▷

To the left, the modern cathedral (1884) dedicated to the Immaculate Conception. To the right, the burning of the boat —in the presence of H.S.H. the Prince Sovereign, H.S.H. the Crown Prince and H.S.H. the Princess Caroline— during the tradional feast of St Devote.

THE CATHEDRAL AND OTHER CHURCHES

The most outstanding architectural monument in Monaco is its own geographical construction — a palace of rocks built on the sea. The best architects have appreciated this natural beauty and built according to the dictates of rock and sea. The cathedral itself is almost a natural complement to the cliffs of Monaco. It arises at one end of the city like the forecastle of a ship looking out onto the sea. The

Church of St. Dévote.   The Rainier III Nautical Stadium.

cathedral was built between 1875 and 1884 by the architect Charles Lenormand.

The churches of Saint Charles and Saint Devote are even older than the cathedral and were built when Prince Charles III fought for the religious independence of Monaco. Until this time, the Principality had been dependent on the diocese of Nice.

THE GARDENS

Situated in a unique area of the Mediterranean due to its climate and its geographical location, Monaco is a country with exotic vegetation of great beauty. Almost every species adapts to this temperature climate, from African flora to Arizona cactus. The Monegasque is fond of fine things and has been able to adapt the needs of urban expansion to the rich ecology of his land. In this, as in many other matters, this small country can be considered to be in the forefront of ecological awareness. And it is thanks to this awareness that life here is fresh and spontaneous, full of gaiety and colour, in a privileged country that can boast at the same time of being in

The beautiful wide bay opens out beneath the Exotic Garden, at a height of more than 120 metres.

Overall view of the Principality.

the forefront of progress and civilization. This is probably one of the most attractive paradoxes of Monaco: its capacity for preserving its history without growing old for conserving its "wild" life while ever mindful of modernity, civic order and exemplary civilization. Like the diamond and the rose, it is the product of spontaneity and order at the same time.

THE EXOTIC GARDEN

The Exotic Garden in Monaco is one of the natural wonders of Europe. Situated on a rock overlooking the sea and the city at an altitude of more than a hundred metres, it is possible to see, from its steep pathways, an impressive view of the city and the whole of the coast of Monaco.

Prince Albert I had already created a small acclimatization garden on the outskirts of the Oceanography Museum. Thanks to the temperate climate of this area many exotic species became acclimatized. However, in 1913, the garden was transferred to another location on a rocky hillside. This spot, which is wonderfully sheltered from the

north winds and from the Mistral, gradually became overgrown in the course of the years, by the curious exotic plants which can now be seen there.

Opened to the public in 1933 during the reign of the great naturalist Prince Louis II, this ideal spot, situated nevertheless on the same parallel as New York and Vladivostok, possesses a multitude of strange paradoxical samples of vegetable life which thrive thanks to the proximity of the Mediterranean. The Exotic Garden is a genuine museum of flora. Due to an exceptional microclimate the plants have grown to the size which is normal in their native countries, and visitors (nearly 450,000 per year) are amazed to find Mexican cacti and African euphorbias more than 10 metres high in this privileged spot. The vegetation reflects the mild climate of the coast with its lovely clear blue sky.

A highly specialized scientific section is devoted to this service and the Exotic Garden often represents the Principality of Monaco in international flower exhibitions, which confirm its outstanding position among the most attractive garden centres in the world.

The slope of the cliff, sheltered from the winds, allows flowers and other vegetation to acclimatize exceedingly well in the Exotic Garden.

THE ANTHROPOLOGICAL MUSEUM

When refering to the Anthropological Museum, we must once again remember Prince Albert I. It was he who founded the museum in 1902 to house the splendid collection of fossils and prehistoric skeletons he had excavated in the grottos of the Balzi Rossi, (better known today by the name of Grimaldi) on the Italian frontier. These caves were explored for six years and provided many finds for the appreciation of the prehistoric era, including animals now extinct from our fauna (the rhinoceros, the elephant, the reindeer, the bear, etc.) together with two types of human fossils.

Among the priceless pieces on show in the Anthropological Museum are the negro skeletons from Grimaldi cave, which lead us to suppose that Europe was inhabited during the Paleolithic era by some African races. The most recent human type belongs to the Cro-Magnon group. All these skeletons are wonderfully preserved and appear in their own prehistoric context, surrounded by many carved tools.

The pieces found in Grimaldi cave were later increased by the excavations carried out in the quarternary deposit in the gardens of Saint Martin, and by the pieces found in the deep grotto in the Observatory gardens.

The success of these exploratory missions encouraged Prince Albert to create the Human Paleontology Institute which was inaugurated in Paris in 1910. With the help of this institute excavations have been carried out in several prehistoric deposits in France and Spain.

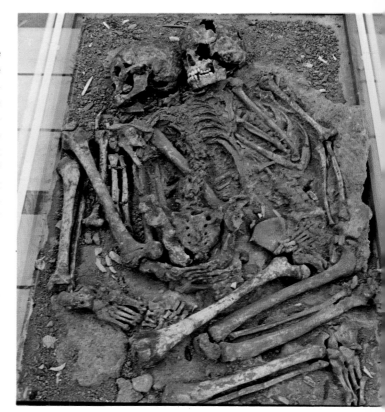

THE WAX MUSEUM

In the magical world of Monaco there had, of course, to be a wax museum. The visitor can find here both history and life transformed into artistic images, as through time had suddenly stood still at a certain point in memory.

The Wax Museum, dedicated to the Grimaldi dynasty («Historial des Princes de Monaco»). Detail of the present reigning family of the Principality.

The impressive, noble façade of the Oceanography Museum rising up above the water. ▷

THE OCEANOGRAPHY MUSEUM

Few countries are as rich, comparatively speaking, in cultural activities as Monaco, with its museums, libraries, theatres, international congresses, and internationally reknowned pedagogical institutions; making the intellectual image of the Principality as prestigious as its touristic fame. In Monaco, things are done properly, continuing the classic Mediterranean tradition which has given humanity some of its oldest institutions. In this country the museums are not merely a gallery of works of art, but rather, genuine institutions devoted to research and study.

This deep and intimate aspect of the Monegasque soul is faithfully reflected in the secluded atmosphere of the Oceanography Museum, an imposing building constructed on a rocky spur close to the sea. The house was designed by the architect Delefortrie, and inaugurated in 1910.

The outside of the building is certainly impressive but even more so is the spirit of study and research to be found inside. The Museum is, in a way, a reflection of

Front and main entrance of the Oceanography Museum, by the architect Delefortrie.

the personality of its creator, Prince Albert I, an eminent man fond of sciences who devoted his life to the progress of culture and the exploration of the sea. Throughout his lifetime he organized four fully equipped ships for research into oceanography, and in these vessels went on some twenty eight scientific trips between the year 1884 and 1914. Prince Albert's

The rooms of the Monaco Aquarium, one of the loveliest in the world.

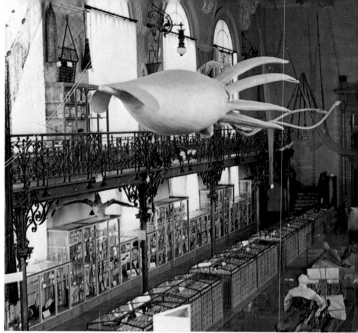

Different views of the rooms in the Oceanography Museum with skeletons on show and the collections made by Prince Albert I during his scientific investigations.

contribution to Oceanography was truly noteworthy; he carried out 3,698 sea explorations, a complete study of the vertical migration of oceanic animals, an analysis of deep sea fauna and of the illumination of the depths, having 2,000 buoys placed in the Altantic to measure the currents, etc.

Besides his discoveries in the Atlantic and the Arctic regions, Prince Albert I built new research instruments and modernized oceanography techniques by using photography and cinema.

Prince Albert created the Monaco Oceanography Museum, and the Paris Oceanography Institute. The best specialists of his time collaborated with him and the Museum soon became the largest European insititution of its kind.

Among the exotic animals that the sovereign himself

caught for the Museum, mention must be made of the famous giant octopus from the Azores, a mythological animal appearing in marine legend.

In his inaugural address, the Prince said, — "I am opening the Oceanography Museum to give it to the servants of scientific truth. There they will find the peace, independence, and emulation that will stimulate their intellect". Since then, the institution has faithfully served the purpose set by its founder. In the rooms of the Museum are the research instruments and zoological specimens collected by the Prince and his colleagues. The scientific activities of this institution are diverse, consisting of marine biology, geology and physics, marine chemistry and physics, cellular neurobiology, applied radio activity, marine radio activity, etc. A notable library, where, besides normal books, there are books of reports on oceanography expeditions, is at the diposal of researchers.

But the section that attracts the largest number of visitors is of course the Aquarium which is one of the largest and most beautiful in the world. The rarest of species can be seen in its tanks, captured from all the seas in the world, including globe fish from Ceylon, damsel-fish from the Philippines and the Red Sea. Some of these species adapt very well to life in captivity and there is a black grouper that has lived there for twenty five years. The visitors to the Aquarium come upon a magical, almost surrealistic world. There are fish of astounding beauty, such as those species inhabiting coral reefs. There are also innumerable strange varieties, such as the gilt head, a fish with a paradoxical evolution, — at the age of 2 it is a male, and after the age of three until death, it is a female. The nature of the octopus is also strange in that it protects the eggs once they are laid with its tentacles until the young are born. Nor must we

The Conference Chamber in the Museum, built by the architect Cavaillé-Coll and decorated with paintings by Hippolyte Lucas. There are several cinema sessions every day to allow visitors to see exciting scenes of deep sea life.

forget the "Preiophtalmes", the most amusing inmates of the Aquarium; these live in and out of the water, chasing insects with expressive mimicry.

To sum up, the Oceanography Museum, emerging out of the sea like Atlantis, borne by a gigantic wave and thrust onto the Grimaldi Promontory as a symbol of our history, is a sort of hymn to the glory of the

On this page and the preceding ones are some of the species of marine fauna on show in the Monaco Aquarium.

sea, in answer, now more than ever, to the express wish of Prince Albert I who declared on the day of its inauguration: "I have donated this as a sort of Ark of the Covenant for scholars of all countries to share in". Aquariums of various sizes, with lighting and installations, the result of specialized studies, have succeeded in achieving an exact reproduction of the natural

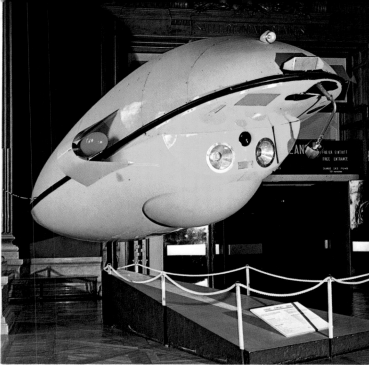

media in which each of the species evolves, allowing the visitor to discover the mysterious life contained in this largest living collection of aquatic fauna in the world. Artists in movement and changing colours, fish and mammals, sea-lions and seals, from the largest to the smallest, all are given the special care required for their acclimatization. A sick bay, out of bounds to the public is open round the clock.

The Oceanography Museum is at present under the direction of the most famous marine explorer of the age, Commander Jacques Yves Cousteau. Thus, in the exhibition and collection rooms, the whaling ship of Prince Albert rubs shoulders with the diving bell known by sailors and underwater explorers alike as "J.Y.C.". In the lecture hall visitors can discover the marvellous world discovered by Prince Albert half a century before through Commander Cousteau's films which are on show continuously. With the Oceanography Museum, the "Scholar Prince" did more than devote the greater part of his life to Oceanography, he stimulated an enormous amount of interest in both popular and scientific spheres regarding the sea.

Besides being the founder of Oceanography, Prince Albert I was also a precursor of Oceanology. Evolution is directing this science to a revaluation of the oceans for the improvement of the human condition. The "Temple of the Sea", a vast construction on sober and majestic lines, with research laboratories that occupy more than 1,900 square metres, directed by the Monaco Scientific Centre and International Atomic Energy Agency, with fabulous collections of shells, and aquariums, dazzling in their beauty and interest, arises like the crystallization of a life entirely devoted to a passion for the sea — the life of Prince Albert I of Monaco.

On the left, the Prince Albert I room evoking the seafaring life of the sovereign and where models of the ships he used on his expeditions and his work laboratory on board L'Hirondelle II can be seen. On the right, one of the modern submarine exploration inventions on show in the Great Hall of Honour.

BEACHES AND PORTS FOR WATER SPORTS

A beautiful country with a marked sea-faring tradition, Monaco has many installations for sailing enthusiasts. The port of Monaco opens out onto the Spélugues Promontory, renamed Monte-Carlo in 1866 by Prince Charles III, and the Monaco Promontory. The Phoenicians, a thousand years before the birth of Christ, had used this port, then came the Greeks and Romans who found shelter here both for trade and conquest.

1866: Monte-Carlo, 1901: the building of the jetties, instigated by Prince Albert I. To this date we can now

La Condamine and Monte-Carlo viewed from the rock of Monaco.

Overall view. To the right, the International Meeting Centre and the Spélugues complex with the Hôtel Loews.

The sea, the skyscrapers, and the mountains in three concentric circles — a characteristic view of the Principality.

add that of the construction of the Spélugues Building Complex at the foot of the terraces of the Casino whose modern aspect fits in perfectly with that of the whole sea shore; this area has been partially reclaimed from the sea and is in the same place as the Monte-Carlo Railway Station and the Clay Pigeon

The terrace with a mosaic by Vasarely. «Centre de Rencontres Internationales».

Shooting Range used to be. In 1975, a magnificent hotel and tourist complex known as Loew's Hotel was added to the tourist hostelries of Monte-Carlo. In the centre of this complex, the Government has constructed an International Meeting Centre — an ultramodern concept to cater for the evolution in

A view of the new districts in Monaco and its careful city planning.

One of the lovely popular beaches in the Principality. New resort complexes are being built on land reclaimed from the sea in the area that was once the Larvotto district.

Fountain 'du Portier.'

techniques required in tourist policy and business activities at the present time.

The International Meeting Centre seen here in the heart of the Spélugues complex and Loew's Hotel, inaugurated in 1978 is the dynamic symbol of Monaco's policy in questions related to business and the tourist industry. Built on a hexagonal base, this centre for congresses has also been reclaimed from the sea. The enormous congress room seating 1,300 and equipped with a stage 220 sq. metres in area, opens out onto the immense blue sea. Exhibitions halls, reception and work rooms, televisions teams and a semiprofessional radio link and... 2,500 hotel rooms in a radius of only 300 metres. This is an ultramodern "instrument"

Apartments, avenues, and splendid resort facilities have been built around the beaches.

which the Principality has incorporated into its tourist and economics policy and placed at the disposal of all congress organizers with its hospitality, beautiful location, quality service, safety and restfulness for tourists and businessmen alike. Its inauguration in 1978 was a milestone in the history of Monte-Carlo.

The main idea in creating the magnificent Larvotto beach was to take advantage of the sea, the sun, and the curiously indented coastline of the Mediterranean in this privileged spot. The main task of the planners was to preserve the quality of the environment. At this they were eminently successful, and the present

The port by night.

Monte-Carlo, and the new Spélugues complex with the Centre de Rencontres Internationales (International Meeting Centre).

Part of the beach.

day coastline of Monte-Carlo not only offers lovely clean beaches but also roads which provide easy access. Flanked by a large avenue that protrudes in the form of a terrace, this public beach stretches for 500 metres with amenities and installations of all types.

A giant car park several storeys high with exits for pedestrians directly onto the sea shore is very near to the beach and opens out onto different parts of the complex.

At the eastern end is the Monte-Carlo Sporting Club,

The beaches on the Eastern shore.

A view of the Monaco coastline.

the scene of the most important artistic and fashionable events in Monte-Carlo, opened in 1974. Beside it is the Sea Club with its private beach, and the Beach Plaza.

Further to the west, going from the Spélugues Complex is one of Monte-Carlo's new luxury hotels, the Hotel Mirabeau. Then there is an attractive centre for indoor sports, varieties, theatre, and exhibitions built in a garden with flowers and trees that look as though they had been there for decades.

Monte-Carlo at dusk.

THE CASINO

The history of the casino constitutes a large part of the history of Monte-Carlo, a district created and integrated in the territory of Monaco.

Scarcely a century ago it was virgin land, a sleepy area on the Côte d'Azur. On some maps, it was marked as "plateau des Spélugues" (plain of caves) because of the underwater caves, "spelunca", that abound beneath its waters. In 1856, the owner of the land sold it at the price of 22 centimes per square metre. No one at that time could foresee the future of the Principality. Its habitants lived modestly from agriculture and fishing. It was difficult to get to the mountain, and the only way was via steep paths that went from the mountain to the sea. Cannes and Nice had better communications and their promotors had already begun to make a profit out of the tourist industry. Lord Brougham made Cannes into a fashionable resort, and in Nice the "Promenade des Anglais" was already under construction. Monaco also needed an exceptional type of administrator in order not to lag behind in the tourist race. This administrator was Prince Florestan, the true creator of modern Monaco.

Prince Florestan was a man of great sensibility as regards the arts and was well acquainted with the world of the theatre; in Paris, he met his wife Princess Caroline who shared his enthusiasm and taste for the arts. Theirs was the idea of making the Principality into a scenario for all types of performing arts and refinements in the art of living. Following the example of the great European spas such as Baden Baden and Marienbad, they decided to open a casino that would be a magnet for the elegant tourist of the period.

The Casino of Monte-Carlo and the lovely gardens decorating this ideal spot in Monaco. (Photographs: S.B.M.).

Prince Florestan's son, Prince Charles III, consolidated the work of his father. The hill beside the bay was chosen for the location of the casino and for the hotels surrounding it. In charge of the gaming rooms was François Blanc, a man with a great deal of experience in this type of business who had already been in charge of the casino at Homburg. Blanc was the creator of the famous *Société des Bains de Mer,* a financial company that not only controlled the administration of the casino but also governed the economic obligations stipulated in its contract which were, to maintain hotels, and organize artistic, social, and cultural activities, etc. Under François Blanc's direction the casino became one of the most famous gaming institutions in the whole of Europe. The habitués of the casino used to say humourously, "whether it's red or black, it's always Blanc (white) that wins".

The district of Monte-Carlo thus became a meeting place for elegant society, a baroque fortress for the potentates of the whole world, city of dreams and jewels, of beauty and flowers. The development of Monte-Carlo went parallel to that of the Belle Epoque, when the predominating note in Europe was one of rounded feminine forms, and it was according to this aesthetic tradition that the opulent Hotel de Paris and l'Hermitage were built.

In 1864, the casino was nothing more than a small mansion whose main room, now restored, is now the entrance of the casino today. Throughout the course of its history the building had to be enlarged five times. The building, a magnificent example of the liberty style, was finished in 1865. The following year the district of Monte-Carlo was created by royal decree: "The lands of the community of Monaco from the stream of Saint Devote and the road known

Different views of the Casino flanked by palm trees and spacious gardens. (Photographs: S.B.M.).

as Franciosi, between the large roadway and the sea shore, will in future go by the name of district of Monte-Carlo". So this was how the tourist paradise of Monte-Carlo was born, star of the night life of Monaco, the permanent heart of elegant society and its meetings at the gaming tables, in the cafés, and in the large luxurious hotels.

Monte-Carlo represents the triumph of sensuality, curves, and a feminine aesthetic. In the rooms of the casino, we can find wonderful examples of decoration belonging to the Belle Epoque, with its warm, imaginative baroque quality and occasional decadence. Nymphs smoking cigarettes, melancholy youths dreaming over a leafless rose, peasant girls picking oranges with an artificial look of countesses dressed up for the occasion... all these exaggerations have their place in this architecture which covers this area like a baroque smoke screen.

A night time view of the Casino lit up together with the stars and the fireworks of the Monaco festivities. (Photograph: S.B.M.).

The luxurious gaming rooms in the Casino. (Photographs: S.B.M.).

The Café de Paris a focal point and meeting place for elegant society. (Photographs: S.B.M.).

The Hôtel de Paris inaugurated in 1864, one of the great palaces that perpetuate the best of Monaco's hotel tradition. (Photograph: S.B.M.).

THE CAFE DE PARIS

Life in Monte-Carlo basically revolves around three nerve centres, — the Casino, the Hôtel de Paris and the Café de Paris. The first Café de Paris in Monte-Carlo was inaugurated in 1865, but it has been changed and restored throughout is long and brilliant history. The architect Demerlé enlarged the building in 1907 and in the twenties, the decorator Vanhamme transformed the interior. Furthermore, in 1960 another decorator, Henri Rigal, rearranged the rooms to fit in the Bowling Club and the Scotch Club. In 1962, it was changed into a Drug-store and gaming rooms thanks to the kind offices of the Monegasque decorator Reinhard. At all hours of the day and night the mechanical sound of the gaming machines can be heard and from time to time the laughing cascade of money falling as a prize to some lucky gambler. The Café de Paris is the meeting place for all the visitors to Monaco. There have been many famous people who

Hôtel de Paris.

The rotunda in the Hôtel de Paris with its beautiful
polychromed glass. (Photograph: S.B.M.).

have come as customers here, and Edward VII when he was still Prince of Wales came every morning to enjoy the ''crêpes Suzette'' which were specially created for this illustrious gastronome.

Mention must be made of Enrico Caruso, Faruk, King of Egypt, Sir Winston Churchill, the Aga Khan, and many not so famous names that have lent prestige to these famous hostelries.

The large dining room in the Hôtel de Paris: the Imperial Room. (Photograph: S.B.M.).

The cooking of the Hôtel de Paris is preeminent in European gastronomy. Below, the "Grill". (Photographs: S.B.M.).

The Belle Epoque *Restaurant in the Hôtel Hermitage evokes the decoration of the Grand Trianon with its pink marble columns. (Photograph: S.B.M.).*

THE GREAT HOTELS

The hotels of Monaco are without any doubt the best in the world. In the Principality there is a network of hotels and restaurants capable of satisfying the most refined tastes. The Hôtel de Paris is indubitably at the head of the magnificent hotel facilities that Monaco offers.

THE HOTEL DE PARIS

Built by Dutrou, the Hôtel de Paris was inaugurated in 1864. Although work was begun the previous year in 1863, just three years before the official founding of the new district of Monte-Carlo. Since then and up to the present time it has always been once of the most luxurious and refined hotels in the whole of Europe, excelling not only in its perfect organization but also in the exquisite taste of its decoration. Aristocrats, important financiers, famous artists and intellectuals, the social élite of the world has stayed and goes on staying at this hotel. A brief look at some important guests is like a short history of the world: the Grand Dukes of Russia, the Emperor of Austria Leopold II, Sir Winston Churchill... writers, painters, musicians, sculptors, film stars, theatre actors, ballet dancers, singers of "Bel Canto", industrialists and financiers, it

All the charm of the Belle Epoque is reflected in the Hall, a delightful winter garden in the Hôtel Hermitage. (Photograph: S.B.M.).

There is a gambling room in the Hôtel Loews among other amenities which ensure perfect service for the visitor. (Photographs: S.B.M./Loews).

would be impossible to mention all of them as the list would be interminable.

Practically the whole of "who's who" uses the hotel as a meeting place.

THE HOTEL HERMITAGE

The Hotel Hermitage, whose picturesque art nouveau façade was built in 1890 by the architect Jean Marquet, is Belle Epoque in style. The dining room, of vast dimensions, is reminiscent of the Grand Trianon of Louis XIV with its rose pink marble columns. Cosmopolitan society meets together in this hotel too, and enhance this justly famous hotel with its presence.

THE MONACO NATIONAL MUSEUM

In almost every country, a National Museum collects together the most meaningful signs pertaining to its history or the most noteworthy pieces belonging to its artistic inheritance. So it could be said that the National Museum is the genealogical tree of a country, its spirit, its image.

The traveller is not going to find statues, friezes, or paintings in the Monaco National Museum. This is a magical country where history is transformed into a happy childhood and large statues become delicate porcelain dolls. The collections of dolls and automata on show in the National Museum are perhaps the largest in the world. They belonged to Madame de Galéa and then to her grandson and heir, Mr. Christian de Galéa who donated them to the Principality. When going through the doors of the Garnier Palace, the elegant mansion where the Museum is housed, there is a feeling of having entered into a fairy story. The automata and dolls live in an eternal childhood of Hans Andersen stories.

The Monaco National Museum remains as a symbol in a world that has so often forgotten that every adult is a child at heart.

CULTURAL LIFE

Monaco is a country with a distinct flair for culture. Its geographical situation has put it in contact with all the great cultures of Europe and the Mediterranean area. The humanistic dedication of many of the Princes of the Grimaldi family has helped to develop in both its institutions and its people, this love for cultural and spiritual values.

Monte-Carlo has a theatre, the Salle Garnier, frequented all the season by a cultured and refined public that appreciates both classical works and the latest creations of the vanguard in art. The Salle Garnier was founded in 1879 and enjoys a well deserved international prestige for the high quality of the artists who perform there.

The Princes' box. Bottom the large fresco by Feyen Perrin. (Photographs: S.B.M.).

Serge Diaghilev founded his famous Russian ballets in Monaco with the dancer Nijinski as the leading figure. In 1932 Colonel Basil and René Blum founded the Russian Ballets of Monte-Carlo, and since then it can be said that the Principality has never lost its place at the forefront of the art of dancing. In the same way, in November 1985, Princess Caroline created the New Ballets of Monte-Carlo. The best dancers of all time have performed in the Salle Garnier, from Serge Lifar to Alicia Alonso. All Monaco moves in an atmosphere charmed with the harmony of dance. There are few places in the world that can offer a better natural décor for the enthusiasts of this exquisite art.

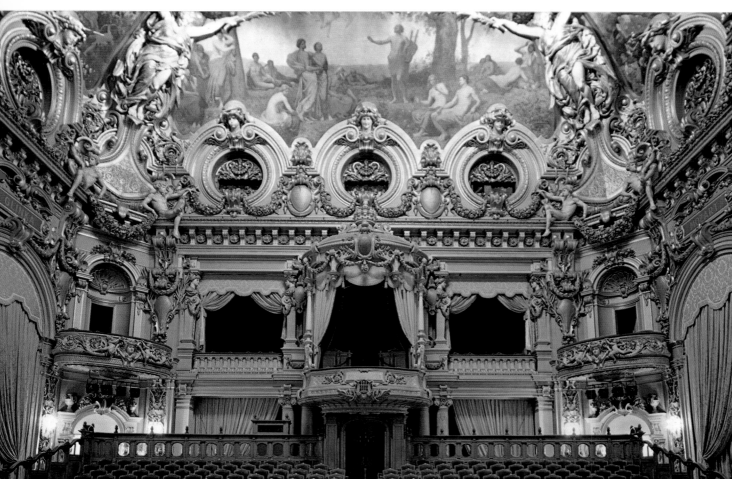

Scenes of the New Ballets of Monte-Carlo.

One of the caryatids decorating the angles of the Opera House. (Photograph: S.B.M.).

An interesting enlarged sample of Monesgasque stamps.

Radio Monte-Carlo in full swing.

There are many things to be seen during the cultural season in Monaco, — cinema festivals, concerts, ballets, exhibitions of paintings, scientific congresses, etc. But none of these activities is organized in an excessive closed or specialized spirit, on the contrary, they provide true enjoyment for the mind and are brought about in a pleasant open atmosphere. We must not forget that Monaco is the country that can change everything into a party.

STAMPS

Monaco is the country of small things, of unforgettable instants, and delicate fragile objects. The Monegasque changes the most elemental and diminutive things into a monument: — the firework festival, a bouquet of flowers, a postage stamp. Monaco is one of the stamp collecting capitals of the world. Its first stamp with the profile of its Sovereign Prince was issued in 1885, and this series with the likeness of Charles III is highly prized on the world stamp market. The first stamp appeared in the Principality in 1725, and H.S.H. Prince Rainier has further enriched the philatelic inheritance of Monaco with a series commemorating the 25th anniversary of his reign.

RADIO MONTE-CARLO

Inaugurated in 1942, Radio Monte-Carlo has become one of the most popular stations in Europe and of course one of the most listened to and most sought after by advertizers throughout the world. R.M.C. is not one but several radio stations. It is a large complex and still expanding, broadcasting 5 programmes in 3 languages: French, Italian and Arabic, not including the other 30 languages used for short wave broadcasts reaching almost round the world. On 1400 metres (long wave) and 220 metres (medium wave), R.M.C. is received in more than 15 countries and sometimes in places very far distant from the Principality, marking its voice heard and communicating its human warmth and international fraternal spirit from the Mediterranean. The miracle of radio waves sends the image and voice of this thousand year old Principality on the Côte d'Azur to lands far distant. These sound waves reach us romantically impregnated with fresh air, the smell of salt and the sea and the perfume of flowers.

Great society life in Monaco, on occasion animated by the presence of Their Serene Highnesses the Princes, takes place at the Monte-Carlo Sporting Club. (Photographs: S.B.M.).

The Gala of the Red Cross in the Monte-Carlo Sporting Club. Fireworks are let off over the sea and from the Star Room, a truly fantastic view can be enjoyed. (Photographs: S.B.M.).

SOCIAL LIFE

The Principality of Monaco has become a meeting place for many social occasions during the last few years: congresses, international conferences, symposiums, etc. The Société des Bains de Mer with its vast experience takes charge of the organization of all these events. In every season of the year, taking advantage of the excellent climate of the Principality, these hotels are disposed to offer their refined hospitality to the traveller. Besides the Casino, the International Meeting Centre and the large hotels, there are many restaurants and night clubs in Monte-Carlo: the Sea Club, the Monte-Carlo Sporting Club, Maona, Jimmy'z, Parady'z...

In summer, the night life centres round the select atmosphere of the Monte-Carlo Sporting Club and the Sea Club. Some modern hotels, such as Loews, belonging to a large international chain, offer the tourist high class entertainment.

In winter, the night life centres around the Casino Cabaret and the elegant dinners of the Hôtel de Paris, in the Folie Russe Cabaret at the Hotel Loews, or at swinging evenings spent at Jimmy'z.

Night Clubs, summer cinema, pools (filled with sea

The Maona, Jimmy'z, Parady'z are some of the many night spots awaiting the visitor to show him some of the enchantment of Monaco by night. (Photographs: S.B.M.).

water, of course)... the Larvotto plain precedes Monte-Carlo Beach. This is a precinct of the Société des Bains de Mer, set up as a private resort whose fame is part of Monte-Carlo's history. With its olympic swimming pool and bathing huts in line along the bay and pavilions scattered along the hill known as "Point de la Veille", with the Old Beach Hotel with its summer comfort, sheltered from the noise of the traffic, the Monte-Carlo Beach is the most distinguished summer club on the Côte d'Azur where, for many decades, international high society has rubbed shoulders.

The fantastic firework display is one of the social events of the season in the Principality.

At the Grand Prix race all the best drivers in the world compete in this daring and dangerous sport.

SPORTS IN THE PRINCIPALITY

An optimistic country forged by the sun and the sea, every aspect of life in Monaco reflects athletic healthiness. The classical inheritance is always present in this luminous corner of the Mediterranean. Here life has the harmonious quality of a work of art and the stimulus of work of business has not been able to break this classical harmony. In Monaco there is always a time and a place for everything, for work and leisure, silence and jollity, for study and sport.

Sport figures high on the list of activities in Monaco. To quote H.S.H. Prince Rainier III whose activity in the sporting world is extraordinarily dynamic and varied... ''to be a good Monegasque you must enjoy sport''.

In spite of the minuteness of its territory, the sports facilities in Monaco are varied and numerous. Thus it is possible to practise almost any sport... except bobsleighing and skiing of course.

With the exception of the swimming pools belonging to the large hotel, tourist, or school complexes, any

swimming enthusiast has two Nautical stadiums with Olympic size pools to choose from. The Rainier III Nautical Stadium, built right in the centre of La Condamine, on the cliff of the great port of Monaco, is often the scene of important international competitions in which several world records have been established, especially the 400 metres free style by the ex French champion Alain Mosconi. The other pool where Alex Jany, another French exchampion set up international records is the one on Monte-Carlo Beach, situated below the Monte-Carlo Country Club.

H.S.H. Rainier III, Prince Albert and Princess Stephanie giving the cup to the winner.

The start.

The competitors on their way through the Casino square with the Hôtel de Paris in the background.

The Vintage Car Rally is one of Monaco's great attractions.

Sports facilities and the ''Rallye Monte-Carlo''.

Also tennis is especially popular and often played in Monaco. The M.C. Country Club has more than 20 courts at different levels in truly lovely surroundings, making it the best reputed club in the world, even compared with Wimbledon or Forest Hill.

Every year in Spring, the most outstanding professional and amateur tennis players in the world meet here to compete in the Monte-Carlo International Championships. Basket-ball, hand-ball, volley-ball, shooting (there is a high class shooting range) squash, fencing, weightlifting, boxing, sailing, and rowing, all have functional modern installations; also the popular traditional game of ''boules'' has its own section in the Rainier III Boule Stand; —in a word— it is possible to be a spectator or to practise all types of sport in Monaco. But there is no doubt that this is one of the most important places for motor racing, as each year two of the biggest championships in the world take place here. The Monte-Carlo Rally, begun in 1911, has become, after more than half a century of history, an event of such importance that both racing drivers and the ''great'' world automobile industry

consider this trial the best publicity asset there is. The first Monte-Carlo Rally took place during the reign of Prince Albert I, the "scholar Prince" with the Frenchman Henri Rougier as the winner doing an average of 10 km per hour leaving Paris at the wheel of a "Turcat-Méry". Since then, the most illustrious names in sport and the automobile industry have appeared among the list of winners of the Monte-Carlo Rally.

The Monaco Grand Prix is a genuine phenomenon and the product of one man's initiative — Anthony Noghes, whose father, Alexander Noghes was one of

The swimming pool of the Old Beach Hotel, included in the Monte-Carlo Beach complex. (Photograph: S.B.M.).

Overall view.

The Louis II New Stadium inaugurated by H.S.H. Prince Rainier in 19/11/85.

the pioneers of the Monte-Carlo Rally, and it continues, in spite of the difficulties in its organization, to be the most exciting Formula I Grand Prix in the world. Thus, since the year 1929 the quiet streets of Monaco have been transformed every year during the festivities of the Ascension, into a special race track attracting more than 100,000 spectators from all over the world.

A sportsman at heart and in spirit, H.S.H. Prince Rainier III has not spared his efforts to foment sporting activities and organize matches and competi-

tions. The Sovereign of Monaco has patronized and instigated practical and ideological movements in sport that have been so well organized that the official representatives of the world of sport have often met together in the Principality to ensure that these events should continue; the International Football Round Table, the European Junior Football Tournament, the seat of the AGFI (the General Association of International Federations) being the most important examples of these.

Sports installations at the Monte-Carlo Country Club.
(Photographs: S.B.M.).

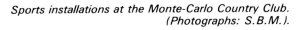

Sailing boats await the sea sports enthusiast.

The waters of the coast of Monaco are ideal for sea sports, from sailing to underwater fishing.

Situated at an altitude of 810 metres, the Monte-Carlo Golf Club is less than 20 minutes by car from Monte-Carlo and Nice. Designed by the famous British player Willy Parks, the M.C. Golf Club satisfies the most demanding devotees of this sport: fairways and greens of high quality, first class installations and facilities, magnificent surroundings and a Club House with a warm and friendly atmosphere. (Photograph: S.B.M.).

HANDICRAFTS

In 1965, H.S.H. Princess Grace established a foundation to help the handicrafts of the country. Her initiative has gone a long way to reviving the old crafts that form part of the historical and cultural inheritance of Monaco. Two stores have been opened for the exhibition and sale of these products made by the foundation. In both these stores (Boutique du Rocher) the traveller will find a large variety of craft work: pottery, paintings, embroideries, clothes, jewels, decorative objects, and the like.

Different samples of the typical handwork of the Principality.

The blazing palm tree rises up above the illuminated port and over the mirror of its water.

EPILOGUE

Scholars state that thousands of years ago, the Grimaldi caves were inhabited. The inhabitants of this period doubtless realized that nature had created a privileged situation here. Centuries have passed by and the sun and the Mediterranean have never ceased to caress the Grimaldi Promontory. Neither the trade of the Phoenicians and the Greeks, nor the war of the Romans, the Spanish occupations or the French Revolution has been able to prevent the existence of the people of Monaco and the sovereignty of its Princes.

Forming part of Mediterranean history, Monaco has always and will always cherish her rights and have her sovereigns recognised.

The name of Monte-Carlo has inundated the mass media — its Opera and the scenario of the Salle Garnier inspired Serge Diaghilev in his creation of the Russian Ballets. Prince Albert built the most famous oceanographic museum in the world and devoted himself to oceanography and scientific research on the sea, long before any committees and ecological associations were begun. Prince Rainier III is at the helm of the new ship of Monaco and directs his craft to the natural shelter that has been built and preserved by his ancestors. A crossroads of the world, the Principality of Monaco is a land where flowers of peace grow. It is a tiny land, of course, but Marcel Pagnol has summarized its social personality in a masterful manner, always expressed through a respect for traditions in which the modern dynamic element is encouraged. ''Here the arts can still live in the shade of the olive tree, close to the Latin sea, there where the authority of one only safeguards the liberty of all.'' Liberty for all. To defend this principle in future time, H.S.H. Prince Rainier can count on his son Albert. The Principality of Monaco will have a soldier worthy of his father and of his ancestors.

Contents

ACKNOWLEDGEMENT:

Our thanks are due to: The Direction du Tourisme et des Congrès, Palais Princier de Monaco, Ministère d'Etat, Société des Bains de Mer, Direction Jardin Exotique, Musée d'Anthropologie Préhistorique et Grotte, Musée Océanographique, Radio Monte-Carlo, Direction de l'Office des Emissions de Timbres de la Principauté de Monaco, Musée de Cires, Galerie d'Initiation Archéologique, Hôtel Loews Monte-Carlo, and the Musée National for their generous assistance, and also to the people who have so kindly contributed to the making of this book.

Collection ALL EUROPE

	Spanish	French	English	German	Italian	Catalan	Dutch	Swedish	Portuguese	Japanese	Finnish
1 ANDORRA	●	●	●	●	●						
2 LISBON	●	●	●	●	●				●		
3 LONDON	●	●	●	●	●					●	
4 BRUGES	●	●	●	●	●	●					
5 PARIS	●	●	●	●	●					●	
6 MONACO	●	●	●	●	●						
7 VIENNA	●	●	●	●	●		●			●	
8 NICE	●	●	●	●	●						
9 CANNES	●	●	●	●	●						
10 ROUSSILLON	●	●	●	●	●	●					
11 VERDUN	●	●	●	●	●						
12 THE TOWER OF LONDON	●	●	●	●	●					●	
13 ANTWERP	●	●	●	●	●						
14 WESTMINSTER ABBEY	●	●	●	●	●						
15 THE SPANISH RIDING SCHOOL IN VIENNA	●	●	●	●	●						
16 FATIMA	●	●	●	●	●				●		
17 WINDSOR CASTLE	●	●	●	●	●					●	
18 THE OPAL COAST		●									
19 COTE D'AZUR	●	●	●	●	●						
20 AUSTRIA	●	●	●	●							

Currently being prepared

	Spanish	French	English	German	Italian	Catalan	Dutch	Swedish	Portuguese	Japanese	Finnish
22 BRUSSELS	●	●	●	●	●	●					
23 SCHÖNBRUNN PALACE	●	●	●	●	●						
24 ROUTE OF PORT WINE	●	●	●	●	●				●		
25 CYPRUS		●	●	●			●				
26 HOFBURG PALACE	●	●	●	●							
27 ALSACE	●	●	●	●	●	●					
28 RHODES	●	●	●								

Currently being prepared

	Spanish	French	English	German	Italian	Catalan	Dutch	Swedish	Portuguese	Japanese	Finnish
29 BERLIN		●	●	●	●						
30 CORFU											
31 MALTA											
32 PERPIGNAN											
33 STRASBOURG	●	●	●	●							
34 MADEIRA											

Currently being prepared

	Spanish	French	English	German	Italian	Catalan	Dutch	Swedish	Portuguese	Japanese	Finnish
35 CERDAGNE - CAPCIR	●			●							

Currently being prepared

36 CARCASSONE

37 AVIGNON

Currently being prepared

Collection ART IN SPAIN

	Spanish	French	English	German	Italian	Catalan	Dutch	Swedish	Portuguese	Japanese	Finnish
1 PALAU DE LA MUSICA CATALANA (Catalan Palace of Music)											

Now being revised

	Spanish	French	English	German	Italian	Catalan	Dutch	Swedish	Portuguese	Japanese	Finnish
2 GAUDI	●	●	●	●	●					●	
3 PRADO MUSEUM I (Spanish Painting)	●	●	●	●	●					●	
4 PRADO MUSEUM II (Foreign Painting)	●	●	●	●	●	●					
5 MONASTERY OF GUADALUPE											
6 THE CASTLE OF XAVIER	●	●	●	●	●						
7 THE FINE ARTS MUSEUM OF SEVILLE	●	●	●	●	●						
8 SPANISH CASTLES	●	●	●	●							
9 THE CATHEDRALS OF SPAIN	●	●	●	●							
10 THE CATHEDRAL OF GERONA	●	●	●	●	●						
11 GRAN TEATRE DEL LICEU DE BARCELONA (The Great Opera House)											

Now being revised

12 THE ROMANESQUE STYLE IN CATALONIA

Currently being prepared

	Spanish	French	English	German	Italian	Catalan	Dutch	Swedish	Portuguese	Japanese	Finnish
13 LA RIOJA: ART TREASURES AND WINE-GROWING RESOURCES	●	●	●	●							
14 PICASSO	●	●	●	●	●					●	
15 REALES ALCAZARES (ROYAL PALACE OF SEVILLE)	●	●	●	●	●						
16 MADRID'S ROYAL PALACE	●	●	●	●	●						
17 ROYAL MONASTERY OF EL ESCORIAL	●	●	●	●	●						
18 THE WINES OF CATALONIA	●	●	●	●	●						
19 THE ALHAMBRA AND THE GENERALIFE	●	●	●	●	●						
20 GRANADA AND THE ALHAMBRA (ARAB AND MAURESQUE MONUMENTS OF CORDOVA, SEVILLE AND GRANADA)	●										
21 ROYAL ESTATE OF ARANJUEZ	●	●	●	●	●						
22 ROYAL ESTATE OF EL PARDO	●	●	●	●	●						
23 ROYAL HOUSES	●	●	●	●	●						
24 ROYAL PALACE OF SAN ILDEFONSO	●	●	●	●	●						
25 HOLY CROSS OF THE VALLE DE LOS CAIDOS	●	●	●	●	●						
26 OUR LADY OF THE PILLAR OF SARAGOSSA	●	●	●	●	●						

27 MORELLA

Currently being prepared

Collection ALL SPAIN

	Spanish	French	English	German	Italian	Catalan	Dutch	Swedish	Portuguese	Japanese	Finnish
1 ALL MADRID	●	●	●	●	●					●	
2 ALL BARCELONA	●	●	●	●	●	●					
3 ALL SEVILLE	●	●	●	●	●					●	
4 ALL MAJORCA	●	●	●	●	●						
5 ALL THE COSTA BRAVA	●	●	●	●	●						
6 ALL MALAGA and the Costa del Sol	●	●	●	●	●		●				
7 ALL THE CANARY ISLANDS, Gran Canaria, Lanzarote and Fuerteventura	●	●	●	●	●		●	●			
8 ALL CORDOBA	●	●	●	●	●					●	
9 ALL GRANADA	●	●	●	●	●					●	
10 ALL VALENCIA	●	●	●	●	●						
11 ALL TOLEDO	●	●	●	●	●					●	
12 ALL SANTIAGO	●	●	●	●	●						
13 ALL IBIZA and Formentera	●	●	●	●	●						
14 ALL CADIZ and the Costa de la Luz	●	●	●	●	●						
15 ALL MONTSERRAT	●	●	●	●	●	●					
16 ALL SANTANDER and Cantabria	●										
17 ALL THE CANARY ISLANDS II, Tenerife, La Palma, Gomera, Hierro	●	●	●	●	●		●	●			

Currently being prepared

18 ALL ZAMORA

19 ALL PALENCIA

Currently being prepared

	Spanish	French	English	German	Italian	Catalan	Dutch	Swedish	Portuguese	Japanese	Finnish
20 ALL BURGOS, Covarrubias and Santo Domingo de Silos	●	●	●	●	●						
21 ALL ALICANTE and the Costa Blanca	●	●	●	●	●						
22 ALL NAVARRA	●	●	●	●							
23 ALL LERIDA, Province and Pyrenees	●	●	●	●	●		●				
24 ALL SEGOVIA and Province	●	●	●	●	●						
25 ALL SARAGOSSA and Province	●	●	●	●	●						
26 ALL SALAMANCA and Province	●	●	●	●	●			●			
27 ALL AVILA and Province	●	●	●	●							
28 ALL MINORCA	●	●	●	●							
29 ALL SAN SEBASTIAN and Guipúzcoa	●	●	●	●							
30 ALL ASTURIAS	●										
31 ALL LA CORUNNA and the Rías Altas	●	●	●	●							
32 ALL TARRAGONA and Province	●	●	●	●	●						
33 ALL MURCIA and Province	●	●	●	●							
34 ALL VALLADOLID and Province	●	●	●	●	●						
35 ALL GIRONA and Province	●	●	●	●	●						
36 ALL HUESCA and Province	●	●									
37 ALL JAEN and Province	●	●	●	●							
38 ALL ALMERIA and Province	●	●	●	●							
39 ALL CASTELLON and the Costa del Azahar											

Currently being prepared

	Spanish	French	English	German	Italian	Catalan	Dutch	Swedish	Portuguese	Japanese	Finnish
40 ALL CUENCA and Province	●	●	●	●							
41 ALL LEON and Province	●	●	●	●							
42 ALL PONTEVEDRA, VIGO and the Rías Bajas	●										
43 ALL RONDA	●	●	●	●							
44 ALL SORIA	●										
45 ALL HUELVA											

Currently being prepared

	Spanish	French	English	German	Italian	Catalan	Dutch	Swedish	Portuguese	Japanese	Finnish
46 ALL EXTREMADURA	●	●	●	●							
47 ALL ANDALUSIA	●	●	●	●							

48 ALL GALICIA

Currently being prepared

49 ALL CATALONIA

Currently being prepared

50 ALL LA RIOJA

Currently being prepared

51 ALL LUGO

Currently being prepared

Collection ALL AMERICA

	Spanish	French	English	German	Italian	Catalan	Dutch	Swedish	Portuguese	Japanese	Finnish
1 PUERTO RICO	●		●								
2 SANTO DOMINGO	●		●								
3 QUEBEC			●	●							
4 COSTA RICA	●		●								

Collection ALL AFRICA

	Spanish	French	English	German	Italian	Catalan	Dutch	Swedish	Portuguese	Japanese	Finnish
1 MOROCCO	●	●	●	●	●						
2 THE SOUTH OF MOROCCO	●	●	●	●	●						
3 TUNISIA	●	●	●	●	●						

The printing of this book was completed
in the workshops of
FISA · ESCUDO DE ORO, S.A.
Palaudarias, 26 · Barcelona (Spain)